I0804476

Classical Guitar Solos

FAVORITE SONATINAS

by David Grimes

The Madagascar Rosewood with Spruce top guitar image on the cover is courtesy of Prenkert Guitars.

WWW.MELBAY.COM

FAVORITE SONATINAS

INTRODUCTION

The early nineteenth century was a time of rapid growth in popularity for the guitar, and guitarist-composers were kept very busy writing music for themselves to perform and for the use of the multitude of amateurs and students. Large numbers of publications offered beginning and intermediate pieces by the acknowledged masters of the instrument, and one of the most frequent forms for intermediate-level pieces was the "sonatina."

Literally a "small sonata," a sonatina can show considerable flexibility of form. It typically has two or more contrasting movements, little or no development of the themes, and a conception generally lighter than that of a sonata. Often such sonatinas were published in sets of three, usually exploring three of the keys most commonly found in guitar repertoire.

The most common sonatina format is in two movements (usually a slow movement followed by a faster one), and the slow first movement serves almost as an introduction to the quicker second movement (most often a rondo). This recipe was used extensively by guitar composers in the early nineteenth century, producing many charming works intended partly for didactic purposes and partly for light entertainment. Nevertheless, composers deviated freely from this pattern. Mauro Giuliani, for instance, used three- and four-movement structures in his "Tre Sonatine," op. 71, but reverted to the two-movement model in "Trois Sonates brillantes," op. 96.

The sonatinas are delightful performance pieces in their own right, but they also serve to help prepare a player for the study and performance of the more advanced and complex works from the period. Just as the Clementi sonatinas have been stepping stones for generations of pianists on their way to Mozart, the sonatinas of Carulli, Carcassi, Giuliani and the others are equally indispensable as preparation for the extended sonatas and fantasias of Sor, Giuliani and Diabelli. Providing excellent training in phrasing and in delineating structures, they are also useful as preliminary steps toward the monumental twentieth-century sonatas of Ponce, Castelnuovo-Tedesco, Moreno-Torroba, Turina, Rodrigo, Berkeley, Ginastera and others.

This collection arose out of my desire to have a one-volume source of sonatina repertoire for intermediate-level students. It has been my experience that the first "larger" form that a student should encounter is the theme with variations, which demonstrates the building of a structure out of smaller, easily digestible sections. Next in order of complexity comes the slightly more complicated and abstract sonatina. For both of these forms the early nineteenth-century guitar composers have left us a wealth of fine compositions, providing ingratiating music with clearly defined themes, phrases, sections and key relationships.

The sonatinas selected for this volume are, for the most part, those that have proven their worth by remaining in the active repertoire until the present day. In preparing the collection, I examined a large number of other, less-known sonatinas and selected a few that I felt were especially useful and attractive.

Working from early editions, I have corrected the relatively few obvious errors and modernized the notation where it helps to clarify musical intentions.

Since intermediate students should be learning to plan their own fingerings (for both hands), I have indicated only occasional fingerings, in general to reinforce concepts and habits of good fingering and in particular to suggest solutions for a few problematic passages.

Composers and publishers in the early nineteenth century preferred to write quarter notes and rests instead of half notes in the bass voice, even where it would appear that the longer duration would be musically desirable. I have retained this notation, but players should be aware that the rests may not be fully intended, and that individual decisions must be made to reflect the specific musical content of any particular passage.

Throughout this repertoire, there are numerous open-string bass notes, and these must, of course, be damped selectively at the appropriate time (usually just after the next note in the same voice) to prevent their suggesting false bass lines or continuing into changed harmonies. In places a chord is followed by an intended rest, and care must be taken to damp any residual open strings. In the last two lines on page 33, for instance, the open third-string G in the C and G chords must be damped to make clean rests. Similarly, in the last two measures of the third line on page 68, the fourth-string D must be damped for each rest.

I am indebted to the Guitar Foundation of America Archives, to the International Guitar Research Archive at California State University, Northridge and to Doctor Mario Torta for helping me locate and consult early editions of these compositions.

David Grimes
June, 1996

FAVORITE SONATINAS

CONTENTS

LEONHARD VON CALL
(1767 - 1815)

The Austrian guitarist Leonhard von Call was born in Vienna, probably in 1767 (although various sources give 1767, 1768, 1769 and 1779 as his birth date), and died there in 1815. A predecessor of the next generation of guitar masters, he would still have been active in the musical scene in Vienna when Mauro Giuliani was establishing himself there as a virtuoso. According to reports from the time, he played the guitar "with unusual skill." He composed many works for solo guitar, for guitar duos and trios, and for the guitar in chamber music.

Most of Call's compositions are light and facile, with little to expand the technical or musical horizons of the dilettante. His "Leichte Sonate," however, offers enough invention and substance to warrant more attention. In three short movements (Adagio - Menuett - Andantino), it makes a fine first sonatina for a student and an excellent introduction to multi-movement forms. This work was praised effusively by Domingo Prat in his 1934 *Diccionario de Guitarristas*, where the movements are described as "developed with impeccable harmonic and guitaristic mastery."

An intermediate student will find few technical problems in this piece, but special care should be taken to keep the pulse steady during the shifts from eighth notes to triplets to sixteenth notes in the Trio.

Leichte Sonate

1. Adagio

Leonhard von Call

fp
calando
p
f
p
V
I
p
f
p
f

2. Menuett

Trio

Da Capo Menuett al Fine

3. Andantino

3
sim.
f
p
mf
₵V
sim.
fp
6

This page has been left blank to minimize awkward page turns.

MATTEO CARCASSI

(1792 - 1853)

Although he was born in Florence, Italy, Matteo Carcassi moved to Paris as a youth, establishing himself there as a guitar virtuoso and a teacher of guitar and piano. Equally popular in London, he made an annual visit to England to perform and teach. He toured frequently on the Continent, appearing annually in many of the larger cities in Europe.

Carcassi's *Méthode Complète*, op. 59, has probably seen more editions, re-editions, revisions and re-publications than any other guitar method. Although much of the technical instruction is now obsolete, the musical examples and studies are still extremely useful. Composed to supplement that method, Carcassi's "Twenty-five Studies," op. 60, are some of the finest studies written for the guitar, recommended and used by the vast majority of teachers today.

The "Trois Sonatines," op. 1, are virtual models of the two-movement sonatina form. Of moderate difficulty, they are tuneful, graceful and inventive. The most problematic passage will be found in the first Rondo (in the last line on page 16), where connecting the melodic line requires close attention to hand presentation and finger substitutions.

In the Rondo of Sonatina No. 2, the last chord in the second stave on page 25 was printed in Carcassi's original as B sharp - D natural - E, which is possible but unlikely. The D sharp seems much more in keeping with Carcassi's general harmonic language and with the rest of the piece.

Sonatina No. 1

1. Larghetto

Matteo Carcassi
Opus 1, Number 1

CVII
sf
sf
p
sf
sf
pp

2. Rondo

Allegretto

IV
②
CV
II
②
①
mf
VII
X
VII
I
③

CI
CIII
CIII
CI
CIII
I
CI

p
CIII
CV
VII
I
ff
mf
p
mf
ff

Sonatina No. 2

1. Larghetto

Matteo Carcassi
Opus 1, Number 2

CV
IX
VII
II
CII

2. Rondo

VI
III
CIII
CI
ȻII
V
ȻV
cresc.
ȻIII
ȻII
II

Sonatina No. 3

1. Andante grazioso

Matteo Carcassi
Opus 1, Number 3

pp
mf
IV
V
IX
VII
IV
II
I
pp
VI
II

2. Rondo

f
III
V
VI
IX
p
II
mf
f

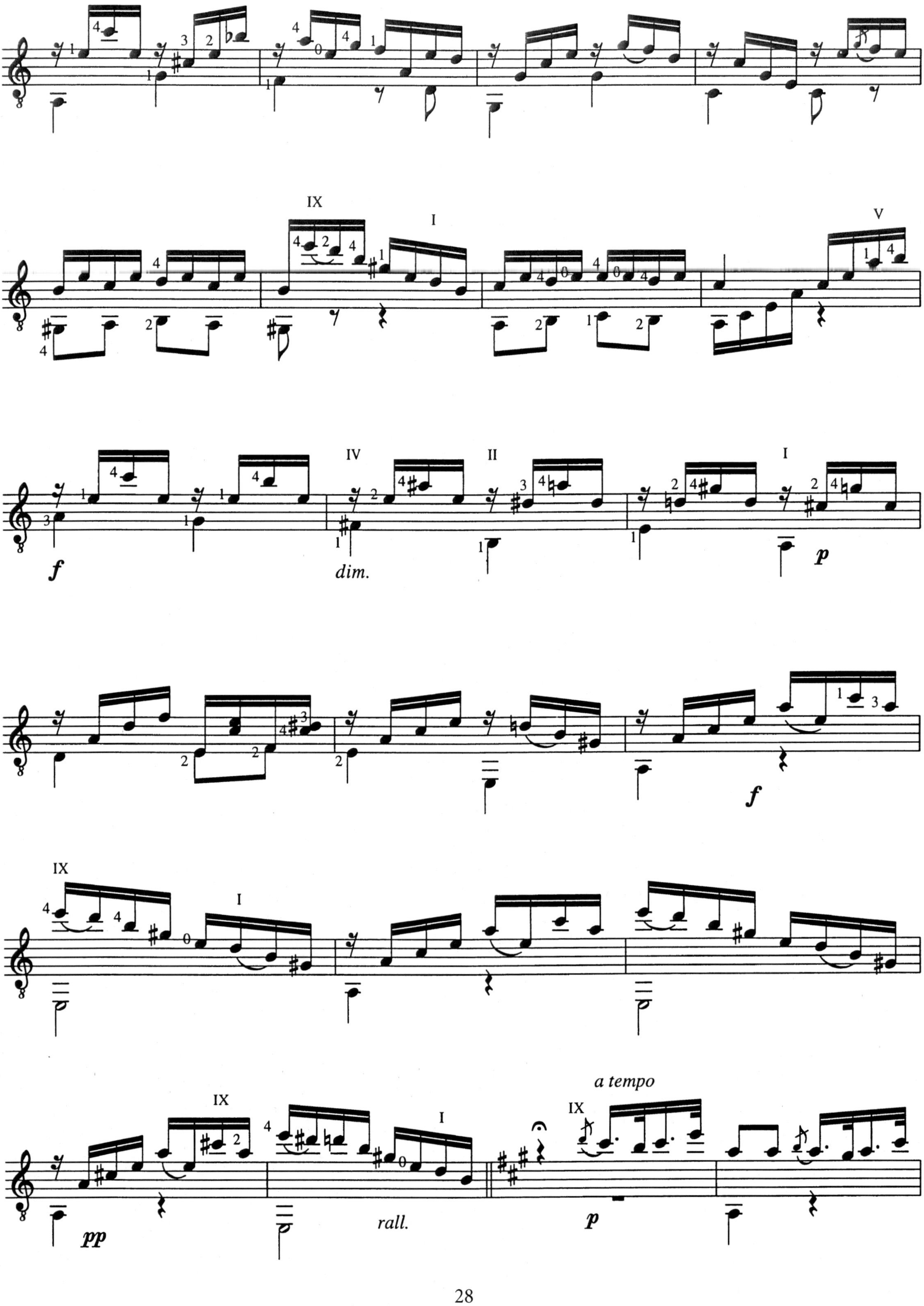
IX
I
V
f
IV
II
dim.
p
a tempo
pp
rall.

mf
p
mf
f
III
p
VI
IX
II
ff
IX
II

This page has been left blank to minimize awkward page turns.

FERDINANDO CARULLI

(1770 - 1841)

A native of Naples, Ferdinando Carulli was one of the "first generation" of performers and composers for the new type of guitar (with six single strings instead of the five doubled strings used on the Baroque guitar). He set about developing an appropriate technique and, as a complementary effort, composed innumerable exercises and studies for himself and for students and amateurs.

In 1797 Carulli moved to Livorno, and then in 1808 he settled in Paris, where he remained a prominent musical figure until his death.

Carulli's catalogue of published works is truly formidable (running to 366 opus numbers, plus numbers of other works without opus identifications). As with so many extremely prolific composers, the quality of writing varies enormously, but his works always show an innate gift for melody, a secure sense of harmony and a solid construction. Traditionally, his compositional output has been most often judged on the basis of his facile didactic works instead of on the more advanced compositions that he and other professionals would have performed, and this has led to an underestimation of his creative ability.

Carulli wrote a number of sonatinas, but the "Trois Sonatines," op. 7, have been the most popular with teachers, students and performers. As in the vast majority of Carulli's works, they contain little sense of conflict or tension, showing instead an irrepressible sunniness and good cheer.

The passage at the bottom of page 34 was apparently intended to lie entirely in seventh position, but a shift to fifth position for the bass C allows a fingering that facilitates a smoother melodic flow.

In the Guitar Archives edition of the "Three Sonatas" (GA 40), the third Sonata includes a second movement, "Andante," that does not appear in Carulli's original.

Sonata No. 1

1. Larghetto

Ferdinando Carulli
Opus 7, Number 1

ff
p
f
p
f
p
f

2. Rondo

VII

f
p
p

m i p a m a m
CII

Sonata No. 2

1. Larghetto espressivo

Ferdinando Carulli
Opus 7, Number 2

IX
Attacca

2. Allegretto

f
p

p
f
p

f

poco f
rinforzando
CII
ff
poco f
rinforzando
ff

Sonata No. 3

1. Largo

Ferdinando Carulli
Opus 7, Number 3

CII
IV
II
CII (hinge)
IV
II
CII
IV
CII
Attacca

2. Allegro

f
p

ff

This page has been left blank to minimize awkward page turns.

MAURO GIULIANI

(1781 - 1829)

Mauro Giuliani was the most celebrated of the numerous Italian guitarist/composers of his time. He was born in Bisceglie, Italy, but spent much of his career in Vienna, where he was in the company of such eminent musicians as Hummel, Moscheles and Beethoven. His frequent performances were received with great enthusiasm and acclaim, and Beethoven is reputed to have been moved by his playing to comment that, "the guitar is a miniature orchestra." A comprehensive biography of Giuliani has recently been written by Thomas Heck (*Mauro Giuliani: Virtuoso Guitarist and Composer*, Editions Orphée, 1995).

Giuliani's music is fresh and imaginative, making good use of the guitar's resources and showing excellent balance of melodic and harmonic ideas. In addition to guitar solos, he composed some of the first guitar concertos, fine chamber works with guitar, guitar duets and many songs with guitar accompaniment.

The "Tre Sonatine," op. 71, have more fully developed forms than most of the other works in this collection. "Sonatine No. 1" features a technically-oriented first movement where the theme is presented four times with figurations advancing progressively from quarter notes to eighth notes to triplets and finally to sixteenth notes. Following this, though, is a graceful "Menuetto" and an especially engaging "Rondo." In "Sonatine No. 2" the second movement again offers a theme varied in progressively shorter note values.

"Sonatine No. 3" is especially noteworthy; constructed from a much more original blueprint, it could be considered a full-fledged sonata. The layout of the movements in the original is not entirely clear in regard to the separation into movements, and the first two are sometimes listed or catalogued as combined into one movement (Andantino sostenuto - Tempo di Marcia). Since the Andantino sostenuto has a full close on the tonic, and because the *da capo* at the end of the Trio certainly refers to the Marcia and not the Andantino, however, I have shown them here as two separate movements. This is certainly the most challenging, and perhaps the most rewarding, of the sonatinas in this volume. It is always an audience favorite and is performed frequently by prominent guitarists today.

The "Trois Sonates brillantes," op. 96, are in the more traditional two-movement mold. Their ideas and developments are concise and elegant, with a good deal of musical invention in a small package.

Sonatine No. 1

1. Maestoso

Mauro Giuliani
Opus 71, Number 1

CI (hinge)
simile
CI (hinge)
CI (hinge)

sim.
p i m a
m a m i
a
m

2. Menuetto

Trio

3. Rondo

Allegretto

3
4
1
1
3
4
2
3
4
3
3
1
2
2
2
2
2
3

III
I
sim.

Sonatine No. 2

1. Andantino espressivo

Mauro Giuliani
Opus 71, Number 2

CI (hinge)

2. Andantino grazioso

p i p i m i p i

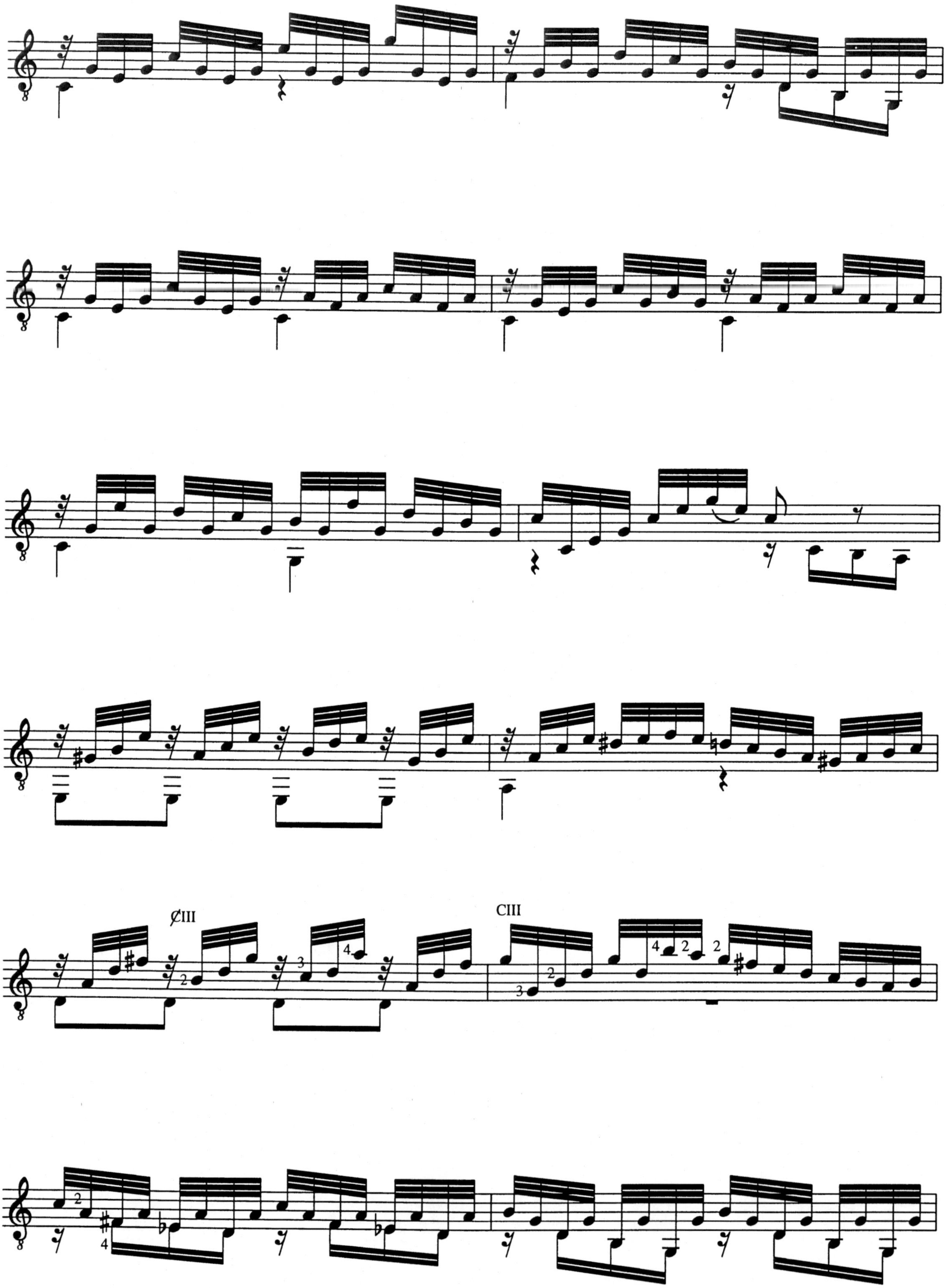
₵III
CIII

3. Allegretto con brio

CII
p
sf

CIII
CII
CI

This page has been left blank to minimize awkward page turns.

Sonatine No. 3

1. Andantino sostenuto

Mauro Giuliani
Opus 71, Number 3

2. Tempo di Marcia

Trio

3. Scherzo con moto

Fine
Trio
Da Capo al Fine

4. Finale

Allegro

V
II
IV
IX

CIII
CIII

VII
IX
II

Sonate No. 1

1. Andantino

Mauro Giuliani
Opus 96, Number 1

CI (hinge)
CI
VIII
CVIII

2. Allegro

CI
VII
p i p i
a
a m a
CVIII
₵III
₵VIII
CVIII
₵VIII
CVIII
CI
₵VIII

Sonate No. 2

1. Grazioso

Mauro Giuliani
Opus 96, Number 2

CIII
f
p
f

2. Allegretto

sf
p
mf
p
mf
p
mf
f
mf
f
ff

This page has been left blank to minimize awkward page turns.

Sonate No. 3

1. Andantino

Mauro Giuliani

Opus 96, Number 3

CIII

mf
p
f
p
IV
mf
V
I
VII
V
I
cresc.
f
p

2. Allegretto

IX
f
IV
V
I
p
mf
f
p
VII
II
mf

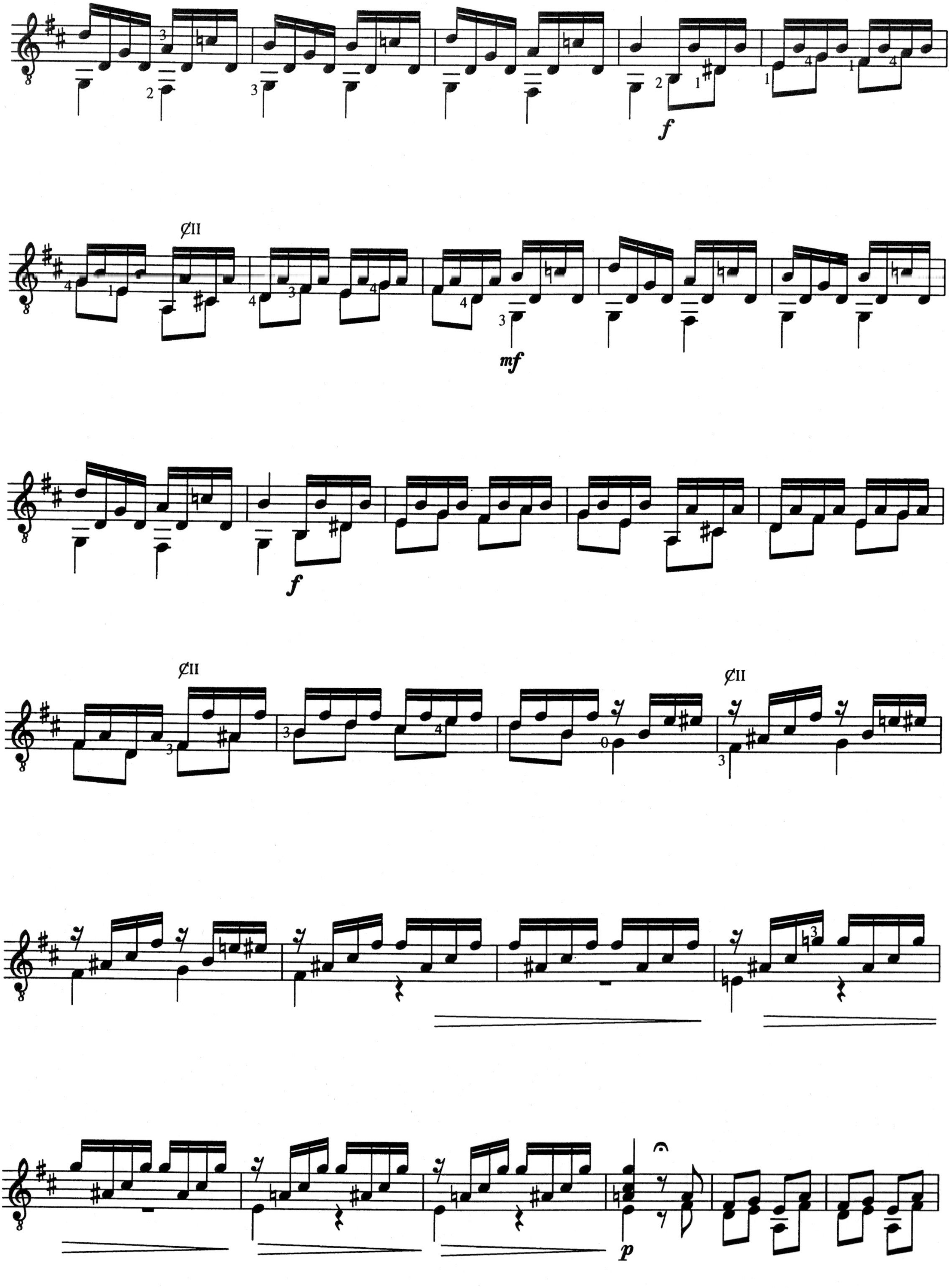
f
CII
mf
f
CII
CII
p

mf
m a m a
i i
f
mf
f
sim.
ff

This page has been left blank to minimize awkward page turns.

FRANCESCO MOLINO

(1768 - 1847)

Born in Ivrea, near Torino, Francesco Molino followed the pattern of so many of his compatriots in developing a reputation in Italy and then seeking fame and fortune abroad. Like Carulli and Carcassi, he finally settled in Paris, where he was respected as a performer, teacher and composer. The popularity of the guitar was immense at that time, and rivalries were bound to be intense. Charles de Marescot's *La Guitaromanie* contains a delightful lithograph depicting (in greatly exaggerated fashion, we hope) a "discussion" that is caricatured as a pitched battle between the followers of Carulli and the supporters of Molino, using their guitars as bludgeons.

Molino's music is skillfully constructed, with lyrical melodies accompanied by effective accompaniment figures. In these three sonatas (especially the first two) the first movements show many characteristics of the sonata-allegro form, with an exposition (contrasting themes in the tonic and dominant), a brief development section, a recapitulation (both themes in the tonic) and a coda. "Sonata No. 1" completes the design with an Andante and a Rondo, and would make a fine introduction to the full sonata form.

On page 104, in the second measure of the last line, the first F sharp was shown as a G in the original. On page 113, in the first chord in line six, the F sharp was missing in the original.

Sonata No. 1

1. Allegro

Francesco Molino
Opus 6, Number 1

₵VII
IV
II
f
p
con espress.

con espress.
¢III
CII

III
V
IV
III
V
VII

2. Andante

3. Rondo

con espress.
rit.
a tempo
VII
IX
VII
V
III
CII

Sonata No. 2

1. Allegro

Francesco Molino
Opus 6, Number 2

CII
p
CII
cresc.
f
ff
con espress.
cresc.
f
dolce
¢III
¢III
sim.

sim.
f
ff
p
p
f
dolce
f
sim.
p
cresc.
f
ff
con espress.

2. Rondo

Allegretto
V
p
f
p
dolce
VII
I
sf
a tempo
ritardando
p
f
p
f
dolce
f
p
f
ff

con espress.
V
CIII
cresc.
VII
Adagio
a tempo

dolce
sf
p
f
ff

This page has been left blank to minimize awkward page turns.

Sonata No. 3
1. Allegretto

Francesco Molino
Opus 6, Number 3

sim.
3
3
p i m a i m p i m

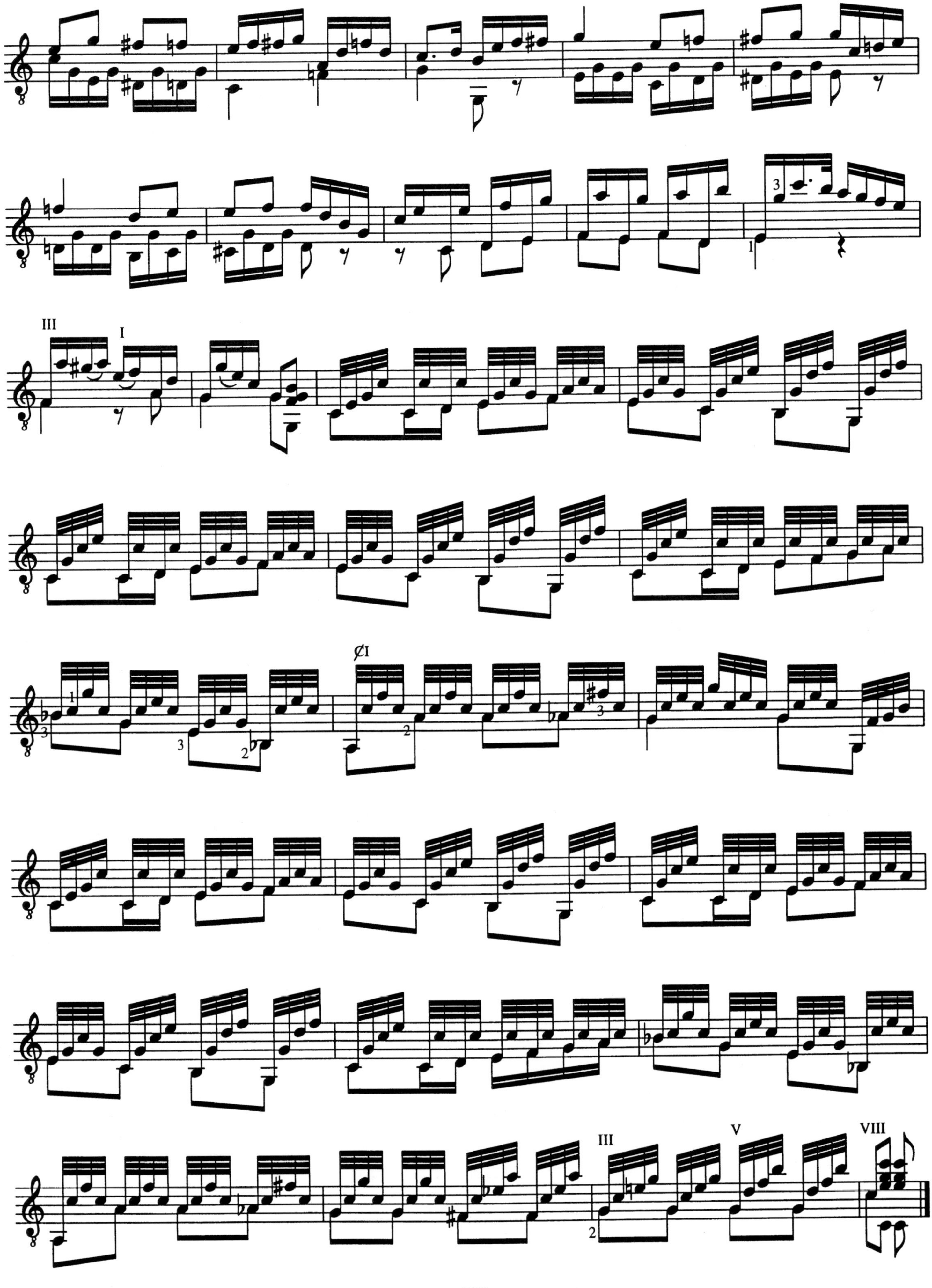
III
I
¢I
III
V
VIII

2. Tema con variazioni

Var. 2

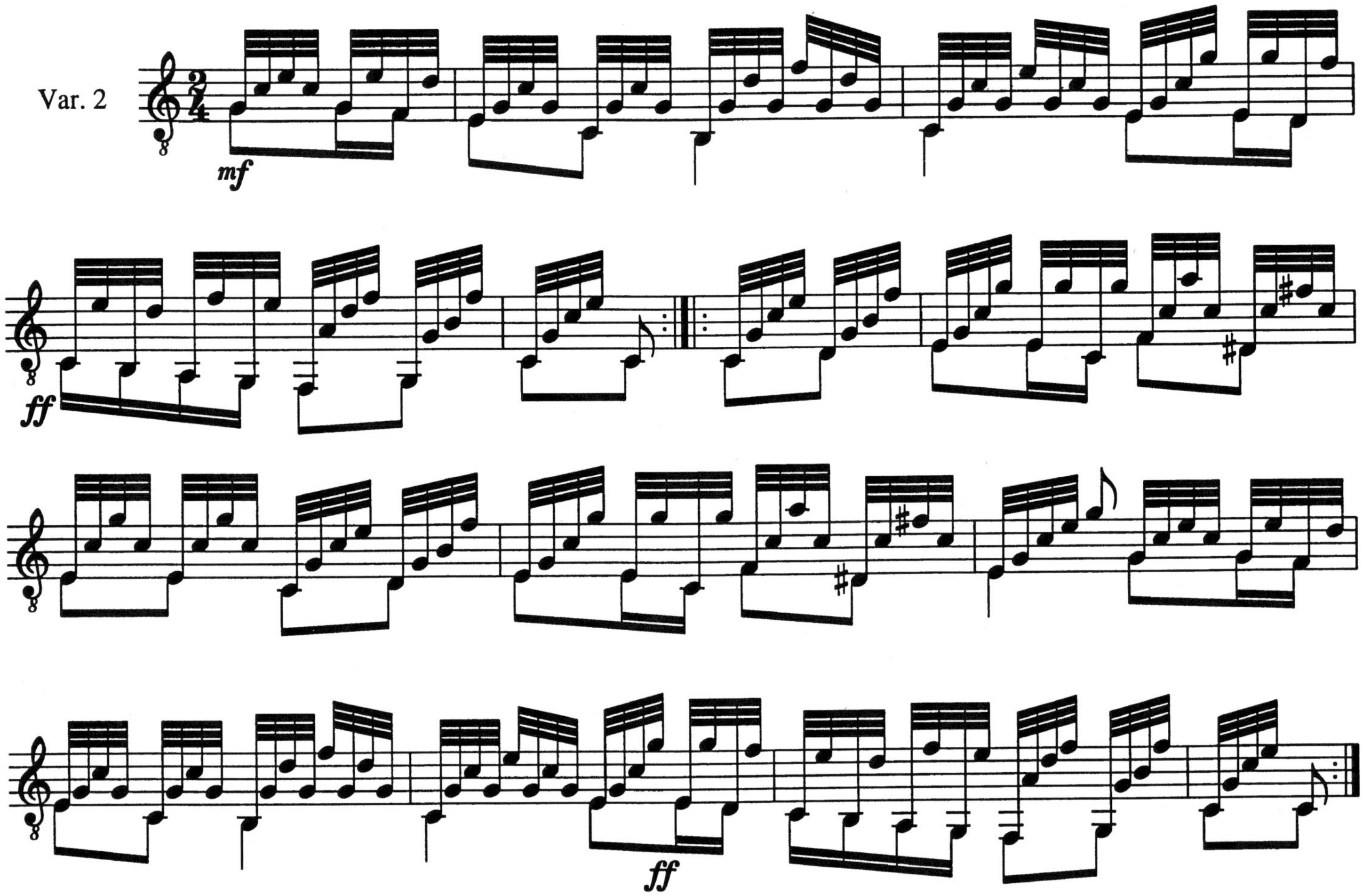

Var. 3

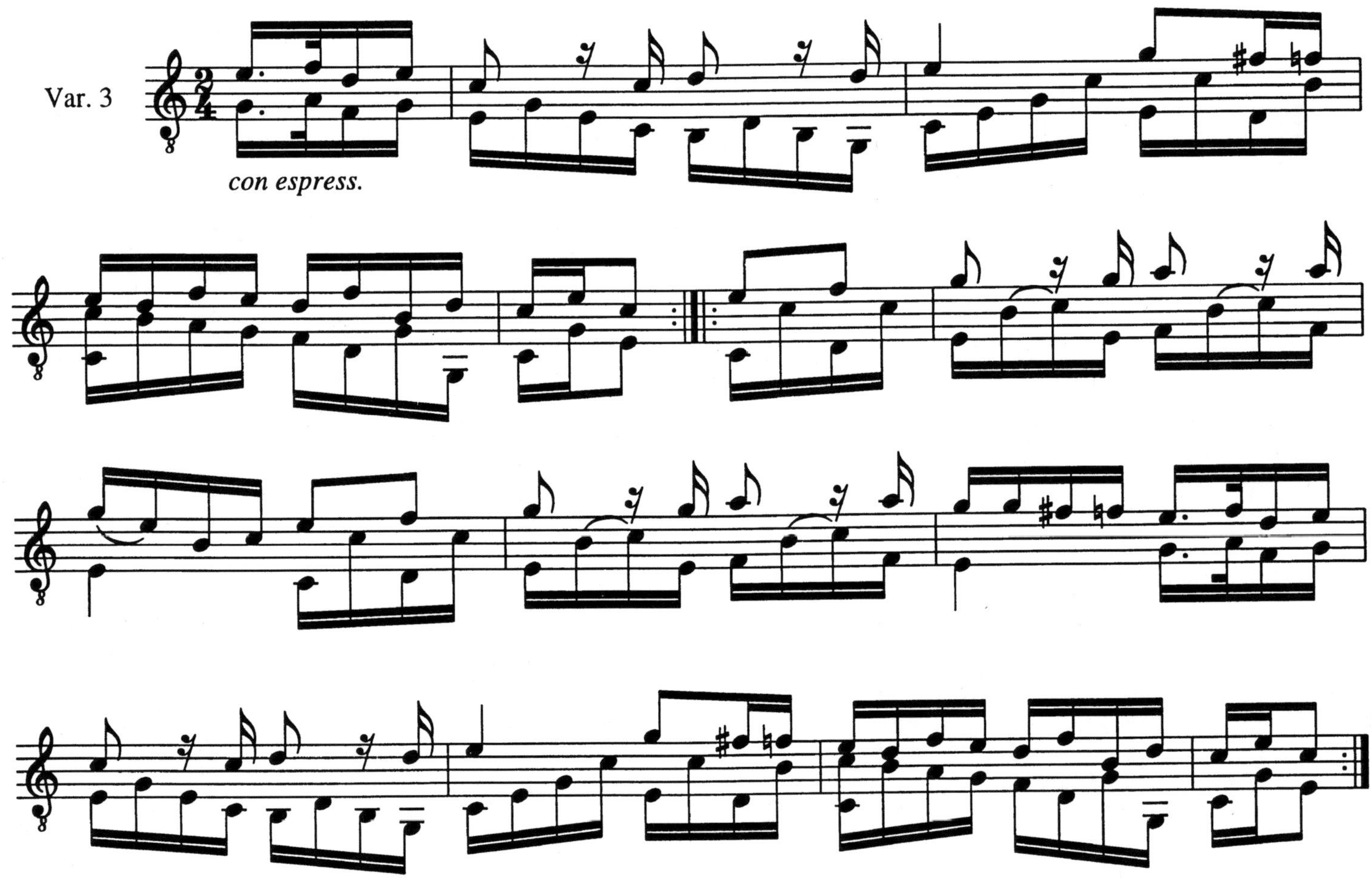

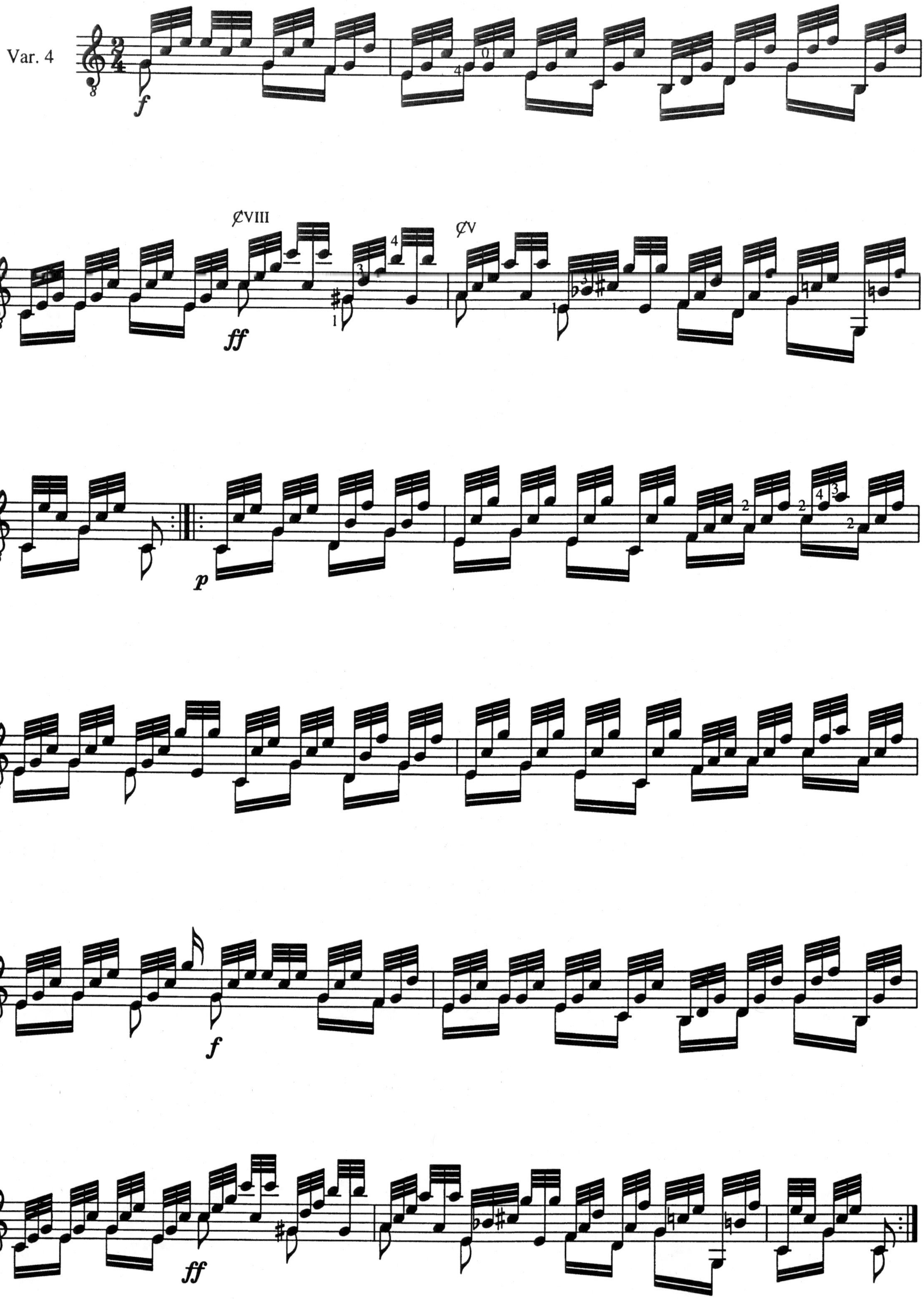
Var. 4
CVIII
CV

ANTONIO NAVA
(1775 - 1826)

Little is known about the life of Antonio Nava, but he seems to have been most active in Milano. He published Methods for guitar, for chitarrone and for archlute, as well as a number of guitar compositions.

Nava's "Le Stagioni dell'Anno" ("The Seasons of the Year") consists of four sonatas suggesting the moods of, respectively, spring, summer, autumn and winter. The programmatic content and the colorful and evocative titles of several movements will help to suggest interpretive approaches:

Sonata No. 1: Spring
1. Cantabile
2. Rondo: The heart exultant

Sonata No. 2: Summer
1. Oppressive heat
2. Refreshing little breeze

Sonata No. 3: Autumn
1. Larghetto
2. Andante mosso
3. The hunt

Sonata No. 4: Winter
1. Adagio sostenuto
2. The cold goes away

"Le Stagioni dell'Anno" was chosen to be the first publication issued by the firm of Giovanni Ricordi (plate 1, dated 1808).

On page 143, the last three bass notes in the second measure were printed as E natural, E, F in the original.

Sonata No. 1: Primavera

1. Cantabile

Antonio Nava

2. Rondo: Il cuore esultante

dolce
1.
2.
dolce
1.
2.

f
p
f
2
4
3
4
3
2
p
f
p
f
f

Sonata No.2: Estate

1. Caldo opressivo

Antonio Nava

Adagio

2. Zeffiretto ristorante

dolce
p

f
f
f
3
3
sim.
3
3
sim.

Sonata No. 3: Autunno

1. Larghetto

Antonio Nava

2. Andante mosso

f
p
f

3. La Caccia

Sonata No. 4: Inverno

Antonio Nava

1. Adagio sostenuto

Mosso staccato
p

3
3
sim.
3
3
sim.
f

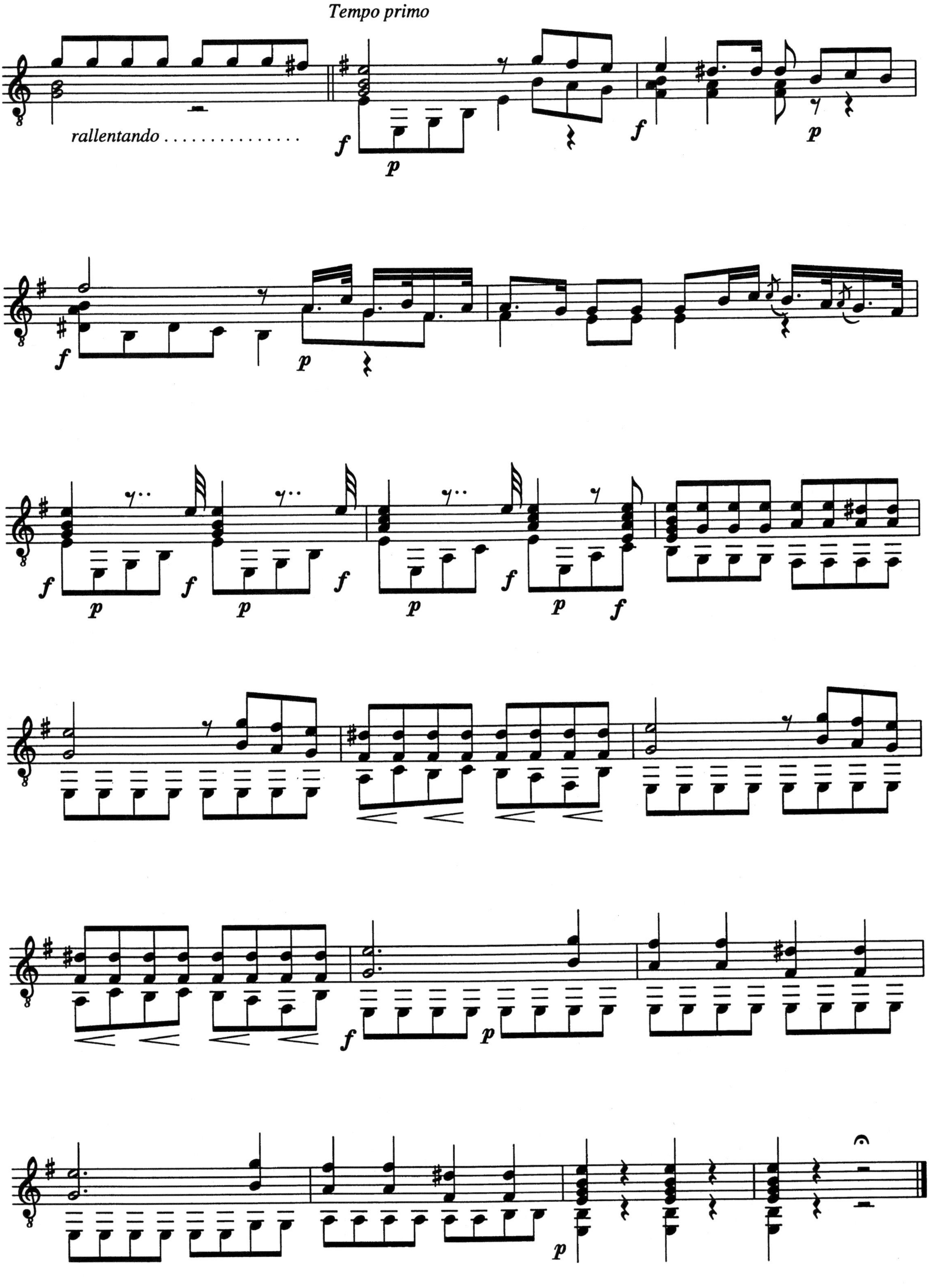
Tempo primo
rallentando . . . .

2. Il freddo se ne va

Allegro con brio

VII
dolce
f

VII

Other Mel Bay Classical Guitar Solo Collections

Other Mel Bay Classical Guitar Solo Collections

Johannes Brahms: Hungarian Dances for Solo Guitar (Estovos)
La Melanconia by Mauro Giuliani arranged by Pepe Romero
Masters of Russian Composition: Alexander Borodin & Antoly Lyadov arr. by Rovshan Mamedkuliev
Padovec Collection (Dojcinovic)
Parlor Gems (Mayes)
Peer Gynt Suite: Op 46 plus Solveig's Song (R. Yates)
Selected Operatic Fantasies of Mertz (Torosian)
Woodland Sketches by Edward MacDowell (R. Yates)
6 Neapolitan Songs for Solo Classic Guitar (Scheldt)
A Dozen Italian Diversions for Guitar Solo (DiBenedetti)
Airs and Ballads for Classic Guitar (Lehmann-Haupt)
Arias for Acoustic Guitar: Operatic Melodies for Solo Guitar (Edwards)
Ashokan Farewell Guitar Arrangement (Ungar/Lehmann-Haupt)
Christmas Songs for Classical Guitar (Castle)
Ciclos: Music of the Sephardic Jews for Classic Guitar (Akiva)
Civil War Suite for Classical Guitar (Brew)
Classical and Flamenco Guitar Solos and Etudes (Elysa Hochman/Jason Hochman)
Classical Guitar Tunes - Fun Solos to Play (Calmes)
Classic Guitar Tunes - Gospel Favorites (Calmes)
Classic Tangos (Halen)
Complete Works of Scott Joplin: 52 PIano Rags, Waltzes & Marches Transcribed for Guitar Solo (De Chiaro)
Contemporary Irish Music for Classic Guitar Solo (Feeley)
Devotion: Sacred Solos for Guitar (W. Bay)
Favorite Hymns for Classical Guitar (Castle)
Five Popular Persian Ballads for Solo Guitar (Afshar)
Five Women Composers Arranged for Guitar (Newman)
Folk songs and Dances of the Jewish People for Acoustic Guitar (Back)
Early American Hymn Favorites for Classical Guitar (Miric)
Great American Marches, Polkas & Grand Concert Waltzes for Acoustic Guitar (Back)
Greek Traditional Music for Acoustic Guitar (Borjanic)
Irish Folk Songs for Classical Guitar (Marsh)
Melodies of the Far East for Guitar (Tuan Vu)
Nineteen Gilbert & Sullivan Favorites Arranged for Classical Guitar (Marrington)
O'Carolan Favorites for Classic Guitar (Böger)
Romantic Arias for Classical Guitar (Eckels)
Russian Folk Songs for Guitar Solo (Borjanic)
Solo Guitar Hymnal: Classic Guitar Solos for the Liturgical Calendar Year (Bass)
Stephen Foster for Classic Guitar (Böger)
The Christmas Book - Carols Arrangeds for Acoustic Guitar (Barreiro)
The Holiday Gig Book (Johnstone)
Traditional Christmas Favorites for Classical Guitar (Siktberg)
Turlough O'Carolan Irish Harp Pieces for Classic Guitar (Böger)
Wedding Favorites for Classical Guitar (De Chiaro)

WWW.MELBAY.COM